Mack and Zack

by Ann Rossi
illustrated by Chi Chung

Scott Foresman
is an imprint of

PEARSON

Glenview, Illinois • Boston, Massachusetts • Chandler, Arizona
Upper Saddle River, New Jersey

Every effort has been made to secure permission and provide appropriate credit for photographic material. The publisher deeply regrets any omission and pledges to correct errors called to its attention in subsequent editions.

Unless otherwise acknowledged, all photographs are the property of Pearson.

Photo locations denoted as follows: Top (T), Center (C), Bottom (B), Left (L), Right (R), Background (Bkgd)

Illustrations by Chi Chung

Photograph 8 ©Dorling Kindersley

ISBN 13: 978-0-328-50697-2
ISBN 10:   0-328-50697-4

Can you see Mack the cat?

Mack can come to Zack.

Can you see Mack the cat?

Mack can have a snack.

Can you see Mack the cat?
Mack can sleep on the mat.

Can you see Mack the cat?
Mack can come this way.

Can you see Mack the cat?

Mack can nap in my lap.

Cats need food and water each day. Someone should brush their fur. Brushing their fur helps cats stay clean. It is good for cats to play and nap. A cat can be a loving pet.